FAILURES OF THE POETS

ANTHONY ROBINSON

CANARIUM BOOKS
MARFA, NEW YORK CITY, ROME

FAILURES OF THE POETS

Canarium Books
Marfa, New York City, Rome
www.canarium.org

The editors gratefully acknowledge
Columbia University School of the Arts
for editorial assistance and generous support.

Cover:
Tobias Verhaecht, *The Death of Aeschylus* (detail, reversed).
Pen and brown ink, brown and blue wash.
Collection of the Metropolitan Museum of Art, public domain.

All other images are by the author.

Design: Gou Dao Niao

First Edition

Printed in the United States of America

ISBN 13: 978-1-7344816-3-1

for Ellis Ruth

Mirth is the mail of Anguish.

— Emily Dickinson

CONTENTS

BUILDER

I always look
for the birds
in your poems
she sd & I sd
this isn't text
speak this is
Creeley speak this
is Pound speak
& I sd watch out
all that etc.
but she smiled
& there was a bird
in my head & a bird
in my back pocket
& the world
was suddenly made
of bridges over low
rivers & these poems
your aviary

MAKING DO

This animal holds a photograph up
to the light, as if the sun will help
to see through what's been written

here, will infuse bit by bit claw, pincher,
furry arm, inky eye, heavy
pink tongue with understanding,

and for what? The spinning
he can't feel but knows is present
in each living thing the magnitude

of our sojourn through this darkest
stretch of afternoon, the millenial
tumult, the hurtle from blank

to black—all part of the design
from which we extricate a shred
of life. A jackrabbit twitches its nose,

cocks back one notched ear and the flight
through the valley dust commences
as it does each evening about this time.

ENGINEER

I am a civil engineer on a crumbling bridge
that spans the lake near the house
where you used to live
growing up in a reed waste fine smooth things
to brighten the interior are spidering
away the life

*

I am a keep in a copse the woods
a reminder of bullets & forks while rattles
clamber outreach in a plastic gallows
forgetfulness does not excuse us rather from
the insides it redeems
giant rhododendron savior of back yards
split fences foment here a resolution
for the scarlet tanager
non-native solutions to overcome
this burgeoning prayerbook
how can we know how to live

FAILURES OF THE POETS

Wyatt couldn't keep count of his "numbrous vers"
And when I mentioned this, a user said, "pronounced properly,
They scan perfectly." They do not, but as a rule,
I've stopped arguing with old men. The shaggy poems,
Derived from an old Italian, have their mincing charms,
And for this he did not deserve hanging, nor beheading.
It's unfortunate to be a human being in the 21st
Century, having learned little to nothing about little
And nothing. But everything is so huge! Battles around
Us, aswarm, and unseen unless one squints hard:
This morning, coming down from LSD, I saw for the first time
A thousand (I exaggerate) small white birds colliding furious
In the wind outside my front window. Flying and crashing,
And on for hours, making their beauty by falling apart;
Do I dissemble? I don't think so. I think sometimes my heart
Is full of inert materials, but I still keep making fragile things.
Whitman was long-winded and too keeping with the rhythms
Of everyday speech—an unpoetic medium—but one must
Only glance back at English Verse to see his rhythms
Were old and honored—he was not encumbered, though,
By regularity, whatever that means. His sister, Emily,
Seemed to know only one rhythm, and that too was just fine.
Nobody genius is ever fine for their time. We would
Do well to remember this. O'Hara was killed by a wayward
Vehicle on a beach in the prime of his life. He enjoyed
Fellating strangers and wrote the most beautiful imperfect
Poems. All of these things are worthy of praise, even the parts
Nobody wants to talk about. Pound succumbed to Italian
Fascism. Like Wyatt, he wandered too far from his native land,

Perhaps, or became disheartened by the brokenness around,
Unable to contain history, he made it himself in a spectacularly
Audacious way, both famous and infamous. And from the ship
I come into this madness too. I cannot hold a job, and have
Birthed nothing significant in this world. I count birds and numbers
Of syllables, but cannot raise my own child. The poems, they
Come as they will. I have a human south of me who loves me,
And I have other ways of being. I will burst into flames, then get up.

CASE MARKER

I like the orange pylon icon I was caddying
for my brother begone a sameness to each
point apart: equidistant hearts blown up
to better see the insides, the gall, appall of
a thing that should know better

*

Been a long fire & now two-dozen mowed
what else? so long night at one time
a sonnet lived here but a sonnet doesn't live here
anymore because we have lost our
capacity to be astonished

*

When this began a wicker broom was enough
or enough to matter to somebody
tinsel & crusting over like a snowbank or eye
reddened to a maddening gone mercury
long road blurred to diminishing saviors

*

Sever fine lengthenings forward to holiday
sanctioned by an animal holding postcards
at arm's length at American expense no
account here or waiting for you flowers disturb
you flower found in a vacant space

*

It's a fiction this new world you speak of an ex-
hilirating bluster of laughter mingled with bigger
roomier corners of shame & this is what I love
about you, brother, sister, ex-wife, this my daughter
my unmaking you my making

ANNIVERSARY

—Memorial Day, 2002

Absent not kissed how much you differ from
my earlier work. These anniversaries
glut: push: disappear where clouds aint floating.
They closed the coffee shop with us still in it.
Seven types of anxiety, clutter, fumble—
Later poems and much later poems and four
kinds of "not"   Does Iowa look like Oregon or away?
You can't rework that thing no more: it's done.

Months later: the poems of Donne, no more, you.
Smiling we swallowed the packets   sugar?
Not kissed, unsolved, not absolved. Our sins make
fools of our circle, our love. October
leavetaking and a sonnet about Milton and bacon,
the breakfast food not the enlightenment man.

BACKYARD

& a prefab interior
for a final

pine tree, thicket
packed with ticks:

water on sound quickens
small child waiting on a train:

standing life a wall
tissue thin: fuse & filament

sparking something
more than minor.

*

More than days, these.

Central casting brought
next to lips

sanctioned
a song

BEREAVEMENT

The mosquitoes have gone to bed because summer
Is dying. Most bathrooms are busy; my father sighs
And heaves upstairs. I feel as if babies are in the walls.

All of this is just for show: crickets and coffee and rivers.
You are the oldest thing in your house. Think about that.

*

There are too many ways of inspecting suffering.
Too many paths to discovering what your mother,
Your cousins, already found. In that garden, there,
Raccoons have toppled a birdbath. My metal detector
Has found a vast field of keys and keychains,
Canadian currency. All lost things remain lost.

*

My dead friend's widow is sending me a parcel
Which will probably bring both memories
And flowers, neither of which is necessarily a sure thing.
Yet I can't help but send it back out to you.

To spread our sorrow is to reach until it breaks your back.
It's good work if you can get it.

To be self-solipsized. To be underground.
After all, it's still just water, extending its mirror for miles.

IN AMHERST

Emily stands in her standard plain frock at the edge of a normal wood, earbuds in, Carlo at her side. She leans down and nuzzles the dog, removes her sneaker, inverts it to free the pebble inside, replaces it on her foot. With great deliberateness, then, she plunges forward into the rust-colored copse, swaying slightly to Mazzy Star, thinking about volcanoes and judges, inhabiting a vague idea of posterity, stopping here and there to admire a thrush or the ridiculous woodpecker. She is walking with her dog in a park in wide-open Massachusetts, as she postulates theorems about gigantic worlds that endure enclosed in domestic spaces.

I WILL TAKE YOUR DEAD

and deploy them far beyond the bluish mountains
and green dark lakes, lichened trees, because I have
no substance of my own. Isn't it queer, little one?
That we find ourselves immaterial. Someone said
render aid, someone said "esprit de corps" and I thought
it meant the soul leaving the body but I misunderstood;
it really meant "Go Team!" Needless to say,
it fractured my sensibilities—the Lord is my beam
splitter, my lumberjack, my Jewish uncle. My father
is dead. He's been dead eight months and the further
I bury your corpses from their point of origin, the more
I feel divested. That word again, that cocooning, body
as clothing, as raiment, as chyrsalis or warp of light.
There is nothing inside. So it is Thursday morning: I
build the fire, I cook the rice, I inject the fat part
of my stomach with a needle full of some shit
from AstraZeneca. Finally I bake the bread.
This is my body, but still I carry yours. I long to be.

FOREIGN OBJECT DAMAGE

We are not driven to belief by sadness,
but to sadness by belief:

occupier on the broken rock wall
that cages a village, two or three young people

gather, mill, outliers in a land of bright plastic,
in this world of coffee cups, zip drives,

& too many fighter jets. Or not enough fighter
jets—it's become so hard

to tell: to tell anything anymore is a grave &
heavy program. Ochre sun, beleaguered former

general, tell me what we need to further wind
down that corridor, what happens in the hazard

lanes. My daughter doesn't ask these questions;
she doesn't have to yet, but it's raining

down to broken. Visibility at an all-time nothing
but "I told you so," & "just shut up and hold on."

MAYAN FACE

Some years ago, I don't know, a half-dozen or so, on the eve of the eve of my leave-taking of my apartment of six years, a man and a woman I'd never met knocked on my door and when I bid them enter, entered bearing beers.

I don't remember their names but the woman lived directly below me and told me she was teaching a geography class that my friend was taking. She was drunk and began to tell me that she knew the schedule I kept, my comings and goings. She knew when I woke in the morning, when I left the building, when I came home, and she knew when I had sex: the building was turn of the last century and the walls were thin. But she told me this. You don't tell strangers this unless you are sure you'll never see them again. Not knowing what to say, I said, strangely, "I guess I've had a good year."

Her man friend handed me a beer and studied my bookcases. He stared at me for longer than is appropriate to stare at anyone you're not planning on beating up or making love to or scolding. He took a swig of his beer and said, reaching out, almost but not touching me—"You have a Mayan face."

They left as suddenly as they had arrived. Outside it was snowing.

POSTCARD

Driving nails through giant hovercrafts of snow
& ice: you there beyond

the rushes, past a semi-circle
of varied thrush and Spanish lessons.

*

Circumference makes fools: shiver on
midwest not making anyone safer:

firm ground is ground yet untilled—
"until the end of time."

*

Is only a time or another tradition: other times
alight then fly up at smoke

& mothers in houses on edges of lakes
are stirring & glad to be awake.

GENEVA CONVENTION

for Gabriel Gudding

The enemy is all around you. If you
get caught they'll make you cry.
If you try to escape, they'll
throw water on your shoes. If you leave
well enough alone, they'll poison
your gumbo. If you smell
like an elephant they'll squash
your mice. If you eat zucchini, they'll
over-tumeric the cooking oil,
resulting in jaundice. If you act
like a Frenchman, they'll give you
dollars instead of francs. If you covet
your own wife, they'll smile and bring
you bread. If you come in the sourdough,
they'll kill fifty birds. If you deny
being speckled, they'll refuse
the right to rummage through the rubbish.
If you turn left, they'll take a pair of trees
and bury GM Hopkins between them. If you
die in a poetic way, they'll hire fifty
Greeks to violate you. If you resist, they'll
convert your cries into dactylic hexameters.
If you stay put, they'll send ants
to your sandwich stash. If you eat and gamble
at the same time, they'll put some meat
between two slices of toast. They'll bring you wine.

EMOTIONAL SUPPORT SPARROW

No more obstruction
No more snowfall

No more fallow ground
No more groaning earth

Some mornings, robotic birds
Swallow the ever

Some mornings, puddle-cloud
Reflections

Some mornings, never

WITHER

Sifted winter across blank fields, found
wheat stalks in piles against the floor, the small Ruths
& the small Boazes
& a draught

of something nourishing.

*

Not far from here's a town.

Antler.

Population: unforgiven.

*

Multiplication tables cornered
in a Pee-Chee folder holding over
middle-aged debris—

transcript in Sanskrit of a tiny hand,
a spring day, a broken wheel.

2000 ORCHARD STREET

Once upon a time, I lived on a diet of baked goods, ice cream, strong coffee, and popsicles. I was thin then, too. And happy in the way a man living with someone who no longer loved him could be. The small human taking up our space helped us forget that until trying to forget was more difficult than simply severing ties. When I moved the couch as I was evacuating that old house on Orchard St—a December day much like this one except that it was 20 degrees F. and wild turkeys pranced about the front lawn—I found a pile of popsicle sticks, dozens of them.

TERNS, HERONS, BITTER MELON

All my hair in a Safeway grocery bag
On the bathroom floor

A soul moves in a straight line
Coming back to the point of origin: the aviary of loss.

What's given:

(a few dollars, clinging, three peach pits, head)

What's tallied:

(told, found, abacus beads, feathers for quills)

Today they circle. On Thursday, they form a V.
We've gotten used to the patterns.

Fruit gone bad on the kitchen counter:
The sweet smell like distance.

The distant smell like

ANOTHER DAY IN MAY

Now more coffee and Brian Wilson
And skittering creatures. I've eaten
Tacos for three days straight and Dad
Is still on oxygen. To feel intense grief
Not right now is also to feel guilty
Concerning elements and microbes
What makes a man sick is also
What kills him, what kills a man
Is also what sustains him. Here, love
Is a concept. Mercy is an act
Of unshabby imagination. Mother
Puts out food for the goldfinches,
A famous athlete debases himself
To the applause of at least dozens.
I've been meaning to talk to you about
The shade-tree and all the shade-tree
People who are as exactly as lazy as I
And exactly as beaten down. Surveyors
Are ranging out back, putting posts
In things. All winter we waited
For the sun and now he's here but will
He make it through another year?

HAVING A SANDWICH WITH YOU

My favorite memories of Florida
Are of all the sandwiches I didn't have
When I was there in the winter of 90-91
And the band played Ride the Lightning
And the galley soundsystem played
Lucy in the Sky with Diamonds while
Christmas floated around us: kids on drugs,
Out-of-work electricians, inner-city geniuses,
Would-be nuclear technicians. But
You, G, were not there. Were not even
A known quantity. Scrambled eggs
Happened, though. Also lying flat
On my back on the concrete, waiting
For the earthquakes to come. Also
Nearly thirty years later, lying on my back,
Having fallen off my own house, unable
To move and listening, rapt, to your
Latest sandwich order: cubano, hoagie,
Cheeseburger. Florida is just a dream
To me: Jack Kerouac, your family dog, Jack
And all the coyotes on all the golf courses
In the wang-shaped peninsula. To translate
This into English requires a special type
Of transmitter. Are there beaches in hell?
Being of unsound mind in my 46th year
I couldn't say but this year, two of my friends
Have died too young. I've tried to un-
Sequester myself and have been met
With resistance and pretty women and sharks

Too because it's shark week, though I think
That all of July and August are shark week
But I don't need a bigger boat. I've got a paddle
And your conversations to keep me
Out of harm's way.

EARLY DISPATCH

Monday in America, still Super Great. Love
Is not like this, sometimes only half-great, other
Times not great at all. Looking from here, from
My perch, into distances and quantities: teaspoons,
Farthings, handspan of some random midshipman:
All depths held at bay, not yet departed. Omaha
Is in Nebraska, land of beef and sweet corn,
And there, America is pumping methane into
The sweet air, fracking fossil fuels and blessing
Their browns with sub-minimum wage labor, like
Miniature foreign Herculeses. This is more and better
Than Love, my love. This is the land of the bronzed
But only artificially: white eye holes protrude from
Chopper exhaust-swept hair. Our Raccoon in Chief
Roots around in the trash and loves no one because
He knows better. It's Really Great here: the depths
And distances give buoyancy to my minor horniness,
Give heft to my deficit: by which I mean my pockets.
Women of America, hear me: Don't you wish you
Had as many pockets as I? Don't you want to make
Authentic tortillas with me? There is a wide and grand
Fence around my yard, my country. The contractors
Built it on shaky foundation. My love keeps falling down
Or scaled by forty-year-old interlopers. They say we
Want a revolution, old boy. Nobody wants that. I can
Frolic in the surf, hold starfish aloft to the waxing moon:
In this light, I look just as white as everyone else, my bare
Tawny feet planted firmly in the shifting American sands.
"Even tan, your skin seems white." Friends, let's disappear,

Let's go where the love is, let's Americanize our hearts
With airwaves and gunwales and new partners. America
Is not the place for love: the ground has ground us down.
Once I gathered in an alley with three white men and four
Brown bottles. The police stayed away. This is paradise.

A LOCALITY

Wouldn't say why
over iris, speckled grouse,
a forthcoming
of units, emergent on fidelity.

The field is no longer open:
good is no good no more.

Speak with open mouth & hands
on the varieties of grace
or green grass waving its "hello"
at the lakes, still frozen, churning.

The mouth is a wry line straight:
timeline broken open.
Keep pulling the horizon
closer: may need to call a broker.

Fallow, a systemic corrugation
at work with all these white people.

Did it always work like this?
Has it always felt like this?
A closed system not closed:
just avoiding the hassle.

HYMN

You were a child in Tucson,
You were a wooly mammoth,
You were about to be born,
You were the breaking apart of a rare, fine bird.
You came the closest to disappearing.

I was a cheeky, portable hoaxer,
I had a pebble in my mouth,
I was a bolt of cloth dyed purple and black,
I moved through orchards and fancy shops,
I wore torn pantaloons.

We were prehistoric,
We were staples, clips, and brads,
We had the power of the ravine,
We had Percy Shelley's lock of hair,
We swam with goggles through and past,
We walked on bones, unearthed old chandeliers.

He made us quiet, shut our holes,
He gave bread, fed the mouths of fawns,
He moved on in, insinuated,
He busted up our faces, turned our ducks to swans.

When the world was younger, Oh, and colder so.

FORTUNATELY GONE, THIS MUCH GIVEN

Two decades time erases precisely nothing

Waiting assumes a form

*

First snow of the old year & a small girl, purple Gore-Tex,
penciled-in dog left-hand corner;

all the pretty things are taking up space around the corners of
those mouths

open hijacked agape

at delphinium   bundled in banners
                smokestacks jettisoned

& three dictators died this weekend

O loving used to be   "I wait for you"

*

Would it be presumptuous to re-title this series "Beatitudes"?

On this, the first evening of the Festival of Lights

<plaster, hinge, zinc oxide>

Geriatrics have been released from their lairs.

Courageous tweet is not necessarily the same thing as outrageous tweet.

*

Baruch atah adonai.

*

"A city of candles."

INSENSATE

Bees coming into a closed circle, circumstance

"come runnin' to me"

who says forever or the green glass

just the merest trickle
sunstruck / unfastened

tooth by tooth
the Chancellor & "monstrosity"

To you I'll always cleave   FULL STOP

*

hand over the loot   goddamn begonias

this page is not available   I will not avail each them

each thorn   a separate prayer

toil   on for a final reveal

*

An address label goes here but I hesitate to affix the name to the page more from superstition than from any sense of privacy or respect for the dignity of others & besides I don't know how to draw a box in Word.

SMALL POEM

I'm having another one of those days but it's a totally different sort of one of those days than the one of those days I was having the other day because that day was an ALL CAPS day and today I'm not so loud, not so bold, not so sure of my audacity of hope and belligerence of belief because honey, I don't know what I believe in or if I ever really believed in anything except Yoko, you know? Today is like the world is upside down and turtle-green which is a word I learned from a children's book my daughter was reading to me and it was a book about a bear who lived in a house on a beach near the sea. The bear wanted, more than anything, a father. This story broke me.

SMALL DOXOLOGY

There is no God & so
god settles down around like so

some more goes.

*

Foraging for rocks and food
has dried up.

Late season, late fire.

*

God is "no" & the small
part splaying out sophistries:

four more months' cant.

CLEAWOX LAKE

—Florence, Oregon

Unit so far free
to make entrance on a coyote
a broken

cactus tethered falling
snows of last air   newspaper
ink on the hill

hangs above three grimy clouds
& the best of my love so
more to find

uprooted a sandpaper
-like resonance & jangle
these pockets

combed over tilted to the left
askew army cap she & I
watch from a dune

a line of sandpipers & the lake
a cathedral: evaporation
is how you make salt.

FOUR SPEECHES

*

What, oh what, can love poetry do for us in this late age? Every age is a late age, of course, and ours is no exception. The stones still have their lizards, the illicit lovers their skin and flesh and occasional lichens, those trees over there have quinces, your eyes their flecks of green. Does any of this mean love? Is New York love? Is San Francisco love? Is Topeka love? You are possessed of a large mind and, as a consequence, have many books on your shelf. You will not find the answer in any of them.

*

Aristotle divided rhetoric into three "species"—deliberative, to tell us what we should do in the future; judicial, to tell us what we should do about past actions (this usually entails punishment); and epideictic, to praise or blame or simply sing. Most of our daily speech, whether we acknowledge it or not, is epideictic. I've been plugging away at these little boxes of rhetoric for three long months. They scream different things: "love me," or "love has torn my heart out," or "love has rendered me unuseful like a flightless bird," or "God, I wish I could share your cigarette," or "don't stray too far, you might fall into the beasty seas." Many poems have been written concerning the edge of the world.

*

When I want to be comforted, and I'm out of Scotch, and no warm body will suffice, I turn to George Gordon, Lord Byron's "Don Juan." I love to say the name of the poem, the unexpected "J" that forces the tongue to flatten against the palate. I love the name "George Gordon," and that he had a clubfoot and was chubby and loved both men and women. I love the way young Juan flits about, mad in love and lust and life. One time, I made out with a girl while listening to Whitesnake. Don't laugh. I had holes in my jeans. It was 1986. I was mad, bad, and not a bit dangerous. In any case, the erotic appeal of Whitesnake has waned (in this late age), but Juan is still all right by me.

DECADE (2009)

The cedar waxwing can literally die
From getting drunk on berries

It wears a jaunty helmet & hurts no
Body, though sometimes it swerves

In another life, I wrote about
The rhetoric of violence & the New York School

In order to become a Doctor
Of poetry & beating people up

But I didn't yet have a daughter
Hand-sized spiders hung like inky death

From every window in our cracked
Winter house—outside, wild turkeys

I was walking a slim black dog
And getting drunk on beers & the dark

Was so visible I couldn't see a thing
The animals in their bushes vibrated

With a cool radiance: so much electricity
In snowed alleys, so much sleeping

With sweet mothers, so many moving
Vans scattering our dulcet youth

THE PHYSICIAN

In this dream I had, William Empson bit off a piece of my ear. He was nibbling, looking for a way in, attempting to discern the types of ambiguity I contain. He counted: there were eight. I have one extra from my mom's side. We were intimate, Bill and I, but not in a sexual way. No, it was more like a patient-physician relationship, in which he'd feel my balls, and I'd cough. Then he'd diagnose me. This often went on for hours. The diagnoses were the best part: sometimes I had "hearkening compass" and other times, "falsely, thine." My favorite, though, by far, was "bracelet of bright hair."

UP ONCE MORE INTO PASTEL AIRSPACE

Photographs are only photographs again

when someone else is writing the lapse & between the lapse &
the firing of automatic rifles in the sensible distance of forked
road / tongue & this my cramped hand, eye,

tails—

—homes the body of wood.

*

becomes a would that can't

*

Tapped under this gilt fabric [HOVERING] fuzzing at lines
the faux lines / drippy horizon *my little girl has come home.*

*

There's a scene in which all the bombing airplanes dropping
bombs & bombing people & very old buildings rewind & go
backwards, unbombing, restoring the dead, rebuilding from
rumble domiciles & foundries & art museums.

But it's only an old man sleeping in a chair, TV snowing away.

*

[continual flub or preternatural feeling – make note of this, place in upper left shirt pocket]

* * *

some thought given to syntax reflects a foundation, a fondness
for foundness & for sun,

snow, what a small ever brain must make—

—pushing after a door / a handprint

     sandblasted

*

captured by innumerable murmuring of mastodons

our slow work, our fascination with freemasonry:

*

"We have come to towns & villages & are making little music
boxes, none of which are the paintings of flowers or flowers
until a leftover murkiness emerges."

a mother & daughter
stand on the edge of a pier

at the edge of a lake

& appear

to be tumbling heads
into the same

slope of light

*

Gave E a pink camera & some very heavy, very green books
for her birthday. I have heard tales of cupcakes & noisemakers
as well.

The next day, a swimming lesson.

*

E weighs 27 lbs & is 36 in. tall; this is 14th & 25th percentile,
respectively.

*

meantime, we're *dans la merde*.

88 DAYS

ago my father died &
The world is still broken

Open like a geode, too
Dazzling to apprehend,

Too terrible to come home
To. These are mountains, furred

Over with wildness where
Goats eat with abandon, these

Are more than metaphors
For absence or removal, more

Than half-completed histories.
We don't want to live here

Anymore but we have no other
Home. Here in the wild oregano

We can't touch the wind, we
Can't even see each other.

THEY SAY: "PRAISE A SMALL THING"

They say: "praise a small thing"
but I found a filbert, two acorns
a swarm of thirsty fruit flies
microns

monumentally unpraiseworthy
and less important:

nothing here is small:
a foundation of falling sand
spotted towhees flying
wings making semaphore

get me out of here
get me over

in a soaring way
we've gotten charged
and characterized

the way love meanders

THE IDEA OF "IDEA" AGAINST
THE BANKS OF A GREAT LAKE

Family becomes a notion unchecked, uninked.

A family is caught, yoked in a tree, a big tree. A tree of some
ambition & breadth.

White border surrounds, surmounts, absorbs the surfeit of
wavy lines.

Reducible by half. Reducible to 5 x 7.

Family as math problem. Solvable for ( ).

Idea of the word problem: world collapses again into fangs.
        Dead maples fugue off summer,
concise crystalline stasis, more like an adjunct to next year.

Back porch completely under ice & the family looks like this:
[drawing here]
                    or like this: [drawing here]

The blue line in this notebook is something like a third rail
that someone is consistently falling off

repeated until underlined one too many times; emphasis
becomes dismissal.

Family as ahistorical factoid:

Come armageddon   Come together   Come away
little subtrahend

Omissions are not omissions.

WE ARE CALLING THIS SECTION THE BAFFLER

It's a subset of The Fandangler.

*

Cousin to Boozoo Chavais, third in line to the barber chair
& a free tetragrammaton
all of which is to say:

I CAN'T LIVE HERE ANYMORE

*

Four chambers' echo has grown over-familiar.
We dress in velour & corduroy, daisies in our hair.

Never enough ovens.

*

Sprezzatura is back in fashion but I forgot my coat
which I used to call a Mackintosh

when we still dwelt in Liverpool.

MAY YOU LIVE IN INTERESTING TIMES

The world's just not that crazy, open
And farthest from the sun. Can you
Remember fireflies away from this fresh
Elocution? How many years and tears
And bricks away from Central Station?
It's small here. The oil drums yearn.
Cigarettes and Chevrolets, more birds
Than you could hope for, but all molting,

And then all molten. There's no such
Thing as justice, and God won't bring
Anyone back. This is a comfort: there's
Smoke and smeared fingertips on window
Panes. The ground is covered in feathers,
Caliban gathers filberts. We won't save us.

FEELING MINNESOTA

Because everyone around us is dying,
I'd like to see what Minnesota feels like
and narrate it to my brother Guillermo
who dwells in Florida, among sixth
graders and sun-bleached strip malls,
the crumbling bones of old St. Pete,
but tonight is just like any other night
and that's why I'm in the kitchen,
alone over crullers and an ashy cup,
writing this poem about the uses
for a new heart in a cuneiform script
buried on the banks of the river Over There,
buried beneath a childhood in Caracas,
and then in the damp evergreen forests
of the Northwest. One of my many Americas
is here in this manual, this dizygotic reckoning
because though we've never met, Guillo
and I have a certain sameness of bone. Neither
of us has ever been to Minnesota, nor
been best man at some random Latino's wedding
and because our kin are all dispersed
our words commingled Jenga blocks
in the permanent 1970s radio fuzz that looks
like smoke. It's something we build together,
through remembered songs and new translations
if I'm lying strike me down if I'm lying down
pick me up and hand a brown hand here,
is something I said once, full of acid and harsh light.
But Minnesota is just a place on a flat map

I'm driving to in a car I don't own. I'm fighting
upward because what is it like to be 45 years old
and estranged from the stand of trees, the mud
daubing wasps, the prosperous crows, dropping
their shit on dappled lawns, because my friend
and I are anti-suicide machines. To be alive
in this, the most beautiful atrocity, is to be mortal
and aware of children, of corrugations and ministrations,
to render unto GOD JESUS nothing because we
don't believe in GOD JESUS but we believe
in me. We don't believe in me.

In a long-buried dream we are boys of 8 and 10
in a long and windy corridor, waves of papery flora
brushing our legs and Led Zeppelin is not a thing that exists,
and for that I am thankful. There are throngs
of old people, *abuelos* and *abuelitas*, over
the next hill, drinking beer from brown
stubby bottles, held in their brown stubby
hands. But it's only a rustling
of papers, the hum of the Frigidaire,
and we're back on the tracks, rusty and unmovable.

Guillo, pack me a sandwich, fill it with greens,
converge on the corner of Barrister and Locust,
so we can make it mean a thing. *Make it mean*
a thing. Things like the Great Fucking Lakes
things if repeated enough become bright seeing,
become Minnesotan and brimming
with Scandinavian fury.
                              What loves were you

thinking of when you entered each mark
into the automated system and pressed submit?
What time is now? Look at the brains about us,
all aflurry with dance music and svelte ligatures
making one thing almost touch this poem on the uses
of a new fabric, dyed with canary feather and goldenrod,
this hay-colored parabola in a car with crooked
license plates. We are having tacos with vikings
on the banks of several bodies of water.

We are old.

We can't just die on slabs. We're feeling
enchanted, there are clouds, there's a light,
and a wall, stark with our outlines in chalk,
sandblasted, and when the zombie gets on the radio,
says "send more cops," that's where we are
but we, the long-buried and now renovated
with bionics are still here, waiting

to be called back to day which is now actually
night and to be called back to nightmares
which are actually patchy buck-toothed horses
in this kitchen office. Guillermo has a thing
pasted to his chest and it is bigger than a heart.

Press this red button. Play *Kid Charlemagne*.

ON LOOKING AT SOME CHINESE POETS

Some poets sing
About the heaven and earth
To me they are
Always and only
The ground and the sky

And me, I'm tired of living
And my voice is hoarse
From constant appeals
To the empty sky

Clouds are made of water
But insubstantial
A paler version
Of the horrible sea

And my arms are tired
From all this pointless
Rowing so I stand now
On this middle ground

Dark earth not firm
And I lift my tired arms
Dig in my faithless heels
And get to work

MILAN

We arrived and sat in the garden
Where Augustine bled, prophesied
By sliding knives into books, kissed but
On cheeks, rubbed flannels until sparks
Ignited the animals. Then felt ashamed,
Fell upward, past cumulus. Beyond crystal.

You, soiled anchoress, don't remember
This, can only convulse inside
Your enclosure. I struggle with my type
Faces. This is remembrance: we came
Here for your savior, stayed for that
Grove, each apricot sweeter than the rest.

I COULDN'T HIT IT SIDEWAYS

who hears this hears not
song but a found worthless
hymn wordless
profound & demanding a love
w/ unrest

"when I was a painter"
at one time the road was yellowed
from dropsy trance
mangled chardonnay touch of pear
who hears this not hears hollow

tony don't kill yourself
goofing on a poet
drowning the goodbye past
am's clouds & training
in obsequiousness

commence & make commerce
the farmer's market rained out found
each frond each reed makes
something out of worth show me
how to spell it, trace it, name it.

REPAIR

A year & change before my father died,
he & I were mending a fence; Dad
barely able to stand, hunched,
leaning against the heavy post,
my mother looking on, supervising. I stood
awkward, staring into Dad's parched face,
until he fell slightly back, & I inclined
toward him, managing to hammer both
of our thumbs. I think we both cried out,
blood bursting my thumb like a small bright
balloon, staining the new slat, spilling
against his leathery forearm. Mom
walked by & said "You guys
are a couple of pussies." I held out my
hand. She walked inside to fix
lunch. I had never heard her say that
before. Dad & I gave each other a hard
sad stare. I went to look for bandaids.
The August sun beat down. No tears.

"I AM THE KING OF INFINITE SPACE"

We were young & we were shattered.
We took our lives & we settled down.

"I like your town & your trees & your
bodies of water" the way the music
drains out across a field. No vision here.

The house we built no more
than a maintenance shack. Insect shells.
Dry road. No visions.

I don't believe I understand. God
was happening all at once & even
though we didn't believe, he made us
good in the wind, made us something big

& dead & so comes love, so comes
this anniversary. So comes again
up, empty, open on the face of the waters.

Open across the breadth of the sea.

LOVING THE PARADE

for Patrick Herron

I thought they would answer me—

parade and anchoress,
page and volume, fork and thresher,
vein and leaf and spiny torturer,

—but they lay silent in the grasses of the field.

I tried to pilot a flying machine
to the furthest reaches of my neighborhood.

It sputtered black smoke and shed flakes
of paint on the denizens of 12th Street,

it crashed in a huge white field, it sent
signals to space and felt alone.

I found an identical twin, picked her up,
rubbed the dirt from her face
with a wet finger, gave her a sandwich.

We asked extra questions of the sun
who replied by shining very fiercely.

We poked holes in shoeboxes and looked
indirectly at the eclipse, watched something
fanged and frayed eat up the sky.

It was the crushing feeling, the downfall, the windfall.

We wasted time by shooting birds turned inside out
in a cage at the edge of the immigrant camp.

We shared a cigarette, tallied up our dead,
alone in a city of brightly-colored plastic—

SUNDAY MORNING

A Cara Cara orange and a cup of instant coffee
Thoughts of a hungry ginger cat and a Raven
Given to being quarrelsome. Complexities
Of the sepulchre, and then of the selfie, then
Of the self-defense plea. What does anybody know?
About the child you left behind? About a girlfriend
You abandoned, about how easy it is to blame
The same-day plague. This orange is my flesh, my
Christ. For a non-believer it's all we can do. Coffee
Dark oil tar and beyond the weekend field. Finally
Praying hands know no rest. Nobody remembers
The cathedral on fire. Or Leonardo's shadow,
Toward light, *sfumo* they call it. Nobody smiles now.
I'm making cookies and thinking of flying machines.

APPROXIMATION HUM

Parabola of sighs and spearmint afternoons, blue
Sky and yellow finch, socks full of seed, bury me

In Tavern Gulch with the last men of the morning,
Loaned out from Key West or another haven

For middle-aged racists spouting beautiful words,
Dry apricot, muddled seltzer and seven herbs

About all the dead and gone, national static
Clinging to the smoke-stained drapes, your underage

Siege machines: ballistas and bassinets to spear
And arrow-pierce straight through: the babies are dying.

LYRIC FOR A SMALL APRIL

Because it was the murkiest of months, a long April
unraveling from the top of the year, a scroll
that won't refurl,

because I was a man in my early forties and half-
way across the continent, my father lay
in a hospital bed,

dying or something like dying, and because lungs
were collapsing both literally and figuratively
inside the chest cavities

of so many restless and unrested bodies, because
the rain would only stop between the hours
of noon and 2 pm and because

this went on for days, with few phone calls and fewer
prayers, I in my protracted wisdom, with an air
of finality, walked two blocks

to the Chevron station and bought two six-packs of beer,
sat on the porch, and drank to remember things
in case what came next was an air

of finality and two blocks would not be enough. Because
I wanted to remember the rusted orange trucks
and the weathered sheds full of old metal,

the smell of Winston cigarettes on his breath with vodka
and the sweet blooms alongside butts and cans
on the road in 1978 when a six-year-old me

wrangled a garter snake. Because it was not enough to gut
a fish, to gather wood, to carry an armful of flowers
from one place to another,

to put things in their place. Because when I was adjacent
to a grove of various trees or merely everything
taller than me, smallness was a gift

I bore, holding and giving freely, trucks barreling past
on the highway. Because everyone I loved leaned
against long cars, unaware

of their short lives and their bodies like scarecrows
which to me looked like monuments, which to me
were bright enough to burn.

Because everything including April repeats and the scroll
ends just where it begins, we can now safely conclude
nothing, really. Because the showers

will return next year, and we will all still be alive here,
and there will be no rejoicing, no feasting, no dance,
we will be here, small,

smaller than ever before, smaller than this year, but we will
also be full, fuller than yesterday. Now, when I step
outside to piss on the woodpile

and hear the couple arguing in the trailer across the way
and hear the first birds in the still-darkened sky
and morning has come, and I'm crushing cans

but all is still the same and everything is quieter,
a bit less burnished, I mouth this lyric for a small April,
for everything not yet dead, for what's alive.

AUTUMNAL

We are walking in & out of Jane.
Our crusade was called on account of hail & out
on the plain a gentle knight came bearing
pears, cheap

handbags, a following of thousands.
She makes small pictures with her mouth
& turns the corners inward, aiming at the heart.
The man with bar-hair with light-brown eyes

can't bear
the pencil's cheap testimony—he is typing
as fast as he can. She hands him the paper
towel & the last windmill tilts by itself.

THE NEW WORLD

When I was 25 I wrote a poem
Called "The New World." I was young
And new to poetry, surrounded by
The post-colonial moment, fixated
On bright Mondays and horticulture.
I stubbornly believed in beauty.
I got older but I didn't grow up.
The raccoons rattled the trash cans,
Left half-eaten plums on the porch.
Across the sea, when others died
We lit scented candles, muttered
Two decades passed us by.
Sadness, once beautiful, became despair.
I asked, once again, for a favor. Standing
In a pool of petrol, scattered flowers.
Go back inside; everything is fine.

SIX PHOTOGRAPHS

SLADDEN PARK

I have gone on & gone out, have written a life as big as a whale's head, have put sparks to trees in the window I have loved best & least significantly. These things, you know, come nigh accidental. Speak of the big hated men in the park w/ their dogs. Speak to me of your inabilities. They are my own defects as well. As well & as to you, me, the bright playground bars the color of Chardonnay. My thing here is written, a life that pushes up.

You of big hat & tiny heart, step back. A long hibernation has given the lie to "beauty sleep"; I'm uglier than ever w/ a Velcro-like swath of swarth in the field of my face, broken vessels, & crust in my eyes. I've walked a long plank-like protuberance to the very edge of a small plot of land named Sladden. Here there is the mess of the dogs & the mess of the trees, spilling the greens & browns, looking majestic like really tall tweed.

The way the mid-January light hits those dogs makes the golden retriever look more golden. The daffodils not yet yellow have begun to burgeon up, to struggle through the slick ice on which small insects & medium-sized rodents skate, making miniscule figure-eights. Good morning, good morning.

Past the grass-pocked asphalt, past an expanse of a splash of paint delineating for the bicyclists their tidy paths, past the dark park, past the squirrels & their fur, past the Dari-Mart where young men twenty-something buy their beer, there is a small & lovely person deserving of more love. In this manila envelope is a sheaf of promises. I want a sullen woman to kick me out of her house. To feel better is here too written, not often written w/ enough aplomb.

A poem is a collection of words used improperly. A life is a collection of acts turned against themselves. Depression & alcoholism are frequent features of a life. Poems are the direct fruits of these febrile sometimes fatal conditions. Poems are booze's children; they are the offspring of a spring ill-spent & crushed bones. They are hard, pretty, & sterile like a caryatid. A small bug lands on my arm, a katydid. It's really rather large. This is a report on vitality for the actor Heath Ledger who died this afternoon, who was not yet thirty, who needed life more than life needed him. In a movie about love he wore a big hat, though he was not a hated man. He was a hatted man. God bless him. Selah. The report concludes that he is no longer very vital. Bless him. Bless this park.

Hi, how are you? Are you an electable candidate? Which people do you represent? Are you cognizant of the sky w/ its large knob of butter hanging over the houses in which the citizens live, over the backyards in which small humans swing on swings, over the beds at night in which the humans snore & copulate & read about the sun? Tell me who to make the check out to. I arise & search & search for you.

This is the story of a lawyer in New York City who invited a besotted, bereft, & now unbetrothed friend to her loft, who ended up playing the lead in a Cameron Crowe movie version of her own life. This is a dramatic reconstruction, slaked & littered w/ purple gloaming under a glittering Orion, w/ stars for a belt & a sword pointed at my park, 5,000 kilometers from the feisty attorney, in a small plot of land where names are changed to protect the inoffensive. The best are stolen secretly. You reader, may steal from this book. I drink for her to keep all sanity, paper cup, water, two lead pencils; I am not writing a sonnet because a sonnet is a love poem & this is a poem about not love but abiding devotion to a Platonic ideal. I raise a toast then eat a piece of toast, garlic sourdough toast, for her. For her & for the waning moon, the streetlights in their filth-garlanded bounty of chemical brilliance. Selah.

Feeling desperate for America, I have taken the last train through the last tunnel visible from the Great Bridge of the Great City which cannot be named because greatness eludes us at every corner, on every shoreline, but not in back alleys or boutiques. This is not, however, a magical place. It is ordinary, small, & needful. In that, it has dignity. It may frighten us horribly, it may make us ladies & gentlemen. The conductor has spoken something I cannot hear. I step out into dusk into air like warmed honey.

The park is expansively pregnant w/ my first child, who used to be a boy, but now all reports, dream visions, interpretive body change indicators, & well-meaning opinions more or less have built consensus around the whole girl thing. Bless her, small & soft of head, dealer of tiny kicks & stomach punches. Bless her who can hear me but cannot see me, who can taste the soy milk & textured vegetable protein her mother ingests. Bless her who is in the belly of a woman who is also the park, also the collective of drinkers of paper-bagged cans & players of tennis & dog walkers, also the love & the simple despair that wanders supermarket shelves, that plasters itself on bedroom walls of teenage girls also large w/ inside-baby. Bless her, Lord, & keep her. Bless the child & the fall, my little girl: come.

In the park once green, now frosted over, icing sugared, on a bench a man in brown shoes & black sweater drinks a big-ass

Pepsi from a waxed paper cup & on the bench where hobos lay just yesterday now lies a woman, lightly freckled, torpored, mystery on her brow, legs open, not weeping softly, but falling away from herself. Falling away from her is a mass of black hair, mucus, fluid, & a tiny head. Falling out is shoulders, barely eyebrows, barely nipples, barely hands w/ tiny nails. Falling out onto bloody sheets, falling out into the sun-bleached blackened dazzling world, falling, arriving: Ellis Ruth.

ACKNOWLEDGMENTS

Some of these poems originally appeared in *The Brooklyn Rail*, *Coconut Poetry*, *Court Green*, *EM Literary*, *The Equalizer*, *Gondola*, *Mary*, *Mid-American Review*, *Muse Apprentice Guild*, *Octopus*, *Typo*, *Pine Hills Review*, *Skein*, *Snow Monkey*, *Spoon River Poetry Review*, *The Laurel Review*, *The Iowa Review*, *Heavy Feather Review*, *4 a.m.*, *The Atlanta Review*, *CARVE*, *Churchyard*, *Gulf Coast*, *Keepgoing.org*, *Lungfull!*, *No Tell Motel*, *Three Candles Journal*, *Quarterly West*, *The Tiny*, *Verse*, *ZYZZYVA*, in the anthology *Digerati: 20 Contemporary Poets in the Digital World*, and in the chapbook *Here's To You* (Boku Books). Thank you, editors and publishers.

Much love and thanks to all the people for support and encouragement over the years: Josh & Lynn, Nick & Robyn, Dorianne Laux, Robert Hill Long, Carl Swart, Ellen Cantor, Mike Copperman, Tim Shaner, John Beer, Carrie Moniz, Michele Santamaria, Julia Covert, Felecia Caton Garcia, Mark Lamoureux, Gina Myers, Erica Kaufman, Megan Carson, Jeffrey Morgan, Anselm Berrigan, April Putnam, Karen Ford, Tim VanDyke, Kristin Swetland, Guillermo Parra, Jonathan Mayhew, Kirsten Kaschock, Thayre Angliss, Jessie Prichard Hunter, Jess Mynes, Aaron Riverwood, Mark Weiss, Aaron Belz, Gabriel Gudding, John Witte, Kristin Kelly, Jay Nebel, Jeff Coleman, Sara Coleman, Mike Young, Andy Mister, Charles Valle, Laura Hindley, Marci Carrasquillo, Betsy Wheeler, Janice Pang, Allison Joseph, John Gallaher, Bill Lessard, Steven Dunn, Ezra Tishman, Roland Greene, Justin E. H. Smith, Kristi Wallace, John Schelling Pollock, Kris Hall, Abe Sword, Hannah Tracy, and Dan Jones (for the music).

Anthony Robinson began writing poems while serving in the US Navy in the day-glo 1990s. He matriculated to the University of Oregon, where he later taught, in various capacities, for ten years. He currently lives and writes in rural Oregon. This is his first full-length book.